Empowering Single Mothers on their Journey

C. P. Kumar
Rciki Healer
Roorkee - 247667, India

Disclaimer

While every effort has been made to ensure the accuracy and completeness of the content in this book, the author cannot guarantee that the information contained herein is error-free, up-to-date, or suitable for every individual circumstance.

The author shall not be held liable or responsible for any errors or omissions in the content of the book, nor for any damages, or losses that may arise from any actions taken based upon the suggestions or contents presented in the book.

Readers are advised to use their own judgment and discretion in applying the information provided in this book, and to consult with qualified professionals before taking any action based on the contents of this book. The author disclaims any and all liability or responsibility for any actions taken or not taken based on the information contained in this book.

DEDICATION

To all the remarkable single mothers who have embarked on a courageous journey of love, resilience, and empowerment,

This book is dedicated to you.

You are the epitome of strength, the embodiment of grace, and the unsung heroes of our society. Through the highs and lows, the joys and challenges, you have persevered with unwavering determination.

To the women who discovered the immeasurable strength within themselves, facing the daunting reality of single motherhood head-on,

To the mothers who embraced the profound responsibility of raising a child alone, defying societal norms and carving a path of their own,

To the trailblazers who consciously chose single motherhood, embracing the journey with open hearts and unwavering resolve,

To the warriors who navigate the intricate web of co-parenting, bravely facing the unique challenges and finding strategies for success,

To the silent warriors who battle behind closed doors, overcoming hidden struggles and defying the stereotypes that surround unmarried mothers,

To the women who redefine parenthood, finding both joy and challenges in the beautiful tapestry of unmarried motherhood,

To the courageous souls who embrace independence, relishing the freedom while bravely facing the challenges of single parenthood,

To the widows who walk the path of grief and loss, finding hope and healing amidst the shadows,

To the women who rebuild their lives after loss, rediscovering their identity and embracing the journey of self-discovery,

To the united sisterhood of widows, bound by shared experiences, offering support, compassion, and empowerment,

To the resourceful minds who master the delicate balance of single motherhood and finances, overcoming economic challenges with resilience,

To the empowered mothers, celebrating both the triumphs and challenges of single parenting,

This book is a testament to your unwavering spirit, your indomitable will, and your boundless love. May it serve as a beacon of hope, guidance, and inspiration, illuminating the path of empowerment for generations of single mothers to come.

With deepest admiration and respect,

C. P. Kumar

CONTENTS

PREFACE

In today's dynamic and ever-changing world, the face of motherhood has evolved, revealing a diverse tapestry of experiences and narratives. Within this tapestry, the voices and journeys of single mothers shine brightly, illuminating the strength, resilience, and unwavering determination that accompany their unique paths. "Empowering Single Mothers on their Journey" is a book that celebrates the triumphs, challenges, and hidden experiences of single mothers, providing a comprehensive guide and source of inspiration for those navigating the complexities of single parenthood.

This book is a testament to the remarkable strength within single mothers, showcasing their indomitable spirit and unwavering commitment to their children. It explores the multifaceted aspects of single motherhood, delving into the unanticipated challenges faced by unmarried women who unexpectedly embark on the journey of motherhood alone. Through the heartfelt accounts of unmarried mothers, we discover the power of embracing this path, defying societal expectations and reclaiming the narrative of their own lives.

Within these pages, we also encounter the inspiring journeys of those who chose single motherhood, deliberately embracing the journey with a sense of purpose and determination. Their experiences offer valuable insights and guidance for those considering or already traveling the road of intentional single parenthood.

Recognizing the complexities of co-parenting, this book explores the challenges and strategies that single mothers employ to navigate the intricacies of shared parenting responsibilities. It sheds light on the hidden struggles faced by unmarried mothers and provides a platform for their voices to be heard, dismantling stereotypes and promoting understanding and empathy.

"Empowering Single Mothers on their Journey" also showcases the uplifting experiences of single mothers who thrive against all odds, defying societal expectations and rewriting the narrative of single parenthood. These accounts of resilience and triumph serve as beacons of hope, inspiring others on their own journeys.

The book goes beyond the experiences of unmarried mothers to shed light on the unique path of widows, exploring their journeys of loss, healing, and self-discovery. It delves into the process of rebuilding life after the loss of a partner, offering guidance and support to those who find themselves on this challenging path. The experiences of widows who have discovered their resilience and embraced life again serve as powerful examples of strength and perseverance.

Throughout the chapters, the book delves into various aspects of single motherhood, addressing topics such as redefining parenthood, embracing independence, navigating financial challenges, and building a community of support. It celebrates the achievements and successes of single mothers while acknowledging the obstacles they overcome daily.

"Empowering Single Mothers on their Journey" aims to provide practical advice, heartfelt experiences, and a wealth of resources for single mothers and those supporting them. It invites readers to embark on a transformative journey, one that empowers them to embrace their unique paths with confidence, resilience, and a sense of community.

We hope that the experiences and insights shared within these pages will serve as a guiding light, illuminating the paths of single mothers and empowering them to embrace the challenges and joys of single parenthood. May this book offer solace, inspiration, and practical wisdom to all those who walk alongside these incredible women on their transformative journeys.

C. P. Kumar

Reiki Healer

Former Scientist 'G', National Institute of Hydrology
Roorkee - 247667, India
E-mail: cpkumar@yahoo.com
Web: https://www.angelfire.com/nh/cpkumar/virgo.html

Introduction

Becoming a mother is a profound and life-altering experience, one that is filled with joy, love, and challenges. For single mothers, unmarried mothers, and widow mothers, this journey takes on a whole new dimension. In this chapter, we will explore the strength within these remarkable women as they navigate the path of single motherhood. Their stories are a testament to the resilience, determination, and unwavering love that can be found within them. Through their experiences, we hope to inspire and empower all single mothers on their own unique journeys.

Single Mother

A single mother is a woman who raises a child or children without the presence or support of a partner. This could be due to various circumstances such as divorce, separation, or choosing to embark on motherhood alone. Single mothers shoulder the responsibilities of parenting, financial provision, and nurturing their children, often assuming both the mother and father roles.

Unmarried Mother

An unmarried mother is a woman who becomes a mother without being legally married to the child's father or without a partner. This could be due to a conscious decision to have a child without marriage or as a result of circumstances such as a relationship breakdown. Unmarried mothers take on the responsibilities of parenting and provide for their children independently, regardless of their marital status.

Widow Mother

A widow mother is a woman who becomes a single mother as a result of the death of her spouse or partner. This sudden and tragic loss leaves the mother solely responsible for raising their children. Widow mothers not only deal with the emotional challenges of grief and loss but also step into the role of both parents, providing love, care, and support to their children in the absence of their partner.

Embracing New Beginnings

The journey of single motherhood often begins with a major life transition, whether it be through divorce, separation, the loss of a partner, or choosing to embark on motherhood alone. Initially, the road may seem daunting, as these women face the challenges of raising a child without a partner. However, it is in these moments that the strength within shines through. Single mothers find the courage to embrace their new reality, understanding that they are capable of providing a loving and nurturing environment for their children.

Building a Support Network

One of the key factors that contribute to the success of single mothers is their ability to build a strong support network. Whether it be family, friends, or community organizations, these women understand the importance of surrounding themselves and their children with a supportive and caring community. They seek out like-minded individuals who understand their unique challenges and offer a helping hand when needed. Through this network, single mothers find solace, guidance, and encouragement, reminding them that they are never alone on their journey.

Overcoming Challenges

Single motherhood comes with its fair share of challenges, both practical and emotional. Financial responsibilities, time management, and balancing work and parenting can often feel overwhelming. However, single mothers tap into their inner strength to overcome these hurdles. They become experts at multitasking, learning to juggle various responsibilities with grace and determination. Single mothers are resilient, finding creative solutions to problems and always putting their children's well-being at the forefront.

Nurturing Emotional Well-being

Caring for their own emotional well-being is crucial for single mothers as they navigate the journey of motherhood alone. These women understand that self-care is not a luxury but a necessity. They carve out time for themselves, whether it be through exercise, meditation, pursuing hobbies, or seeking therapy when needed. Single mothers recognize the importance of their own emotional well-being and understand that by nurturing themselves, they become better equipped to care for their children.

Empowering the Next Generation

As single mothers traverse their unique journey, they are not only shaping the lives of their children but also empowering the next generation. These women are role models, teaching their children the values of strength, resilience, and independence. By witnessing their mother's unwavering dedication and determination, children of single mothers learn the importance of perseverance and the belief that they can overcome any obstacle. Single mothers empower their children to dream big and achieve greatness, regardless of their circumstances.

Celebrating Victories

In the face of adversity, single mothers celebrate every victory, no matter how small. They recognize that their journey is not always easy, but they refuse to let the challenges define them. Whether it's a promotion at work, a child's milestone, or simply making it through a challenging day, single mothers take pride in their accomplishments. They find joy in the everyday moments, cherishing the love and bond they share with their children.

Conclusion

The strength within single mothers, unmarried mothers, and widow mothers is a force to be reckoned with. Their journey of single motherhood is filled with challenges, but it is also a testament to their resilience, determination, and unwavering love for their children. Through their stories, we witness the power of the human spirit and the incredible capacity to overcome adversity. Single mothers are not defined by their circumstances but by their strength, compassion, and the endless possibilities they create for themselves and their children. May their journey inspire and empower every single mother on her own unique path of motherhood.

Chapter 2. Unexpected Motherhood
Unveiling the Challenges of Unmarried Women

Introduction

Motherhood is a journey that brings immense joy, love, and fulfillment. However, for unmarried women, the journey of unexpected motherhood comes with its unique set of challenges. In this chapter, we will delve into the experiences and obstacles faced by unmarried women who find themselves on the path of single motherhood. By shedding light on these challenges, we aim to empower single mothers and provide a supportive guide for their journey.

The Stigma of Unmarried Motherhood

Unmarried motherhood often carries a heavy social stigma. Society's judgment and stereotyping can cause emotional distress and feelings of isolation for single mothers. They may face criticism from family members, friends, and even strangers. This stigma can lead to a loss of self-esteem and a sense of shame, making it difficult for unmarried mothers to fully embrace their role.

Financial Struggles

One of the most significant challenges faced by unmarried mothers is financial instability. Raising a child alone requires a substantial financial commitment, and single mothers often find themselves struggling to make ends meet. Many unmarried mothers face limited job opportunities due to the responsibilities of parenting, lack of support, and the absence of a partner to share the financial burden. This financial strain can lead to stress, anxiety, and a constant struggle to provide for both themselves and their children.

Lack of Emotional Support

Navigating the journey of motherhood without a partner can be emotionally taxing. Unmarried mothers often lack the emotional support that comes with having a partner by their side. The absence of a co-parent can result in feelings of loneliness, overwhelm, and exhaustion. Single mothers may also experience a sense of grief for the loss of the envisioned family structure, making it crucial to address their emotional well-being and provide avenues for support and connection.

Balancing Parenting and Personal Growth

Being a single mother means taking on multiple roles and responsibilities simultaneously. Unmarried mothers often find themselves struggling to strike a balance between their parenting duties and personal growth. The demands of raising a child can leave little time and energy for self-care, pursuing education, or advancing in their careers. Single mothers need support systems that allow them to prioritize their personal growth alongside their parenting responsibilities.

Co-Parenting Challenges

In cases where the child's father is involved, co-parenting can present its own set of challenges. Communication breakdowns, disagreements over parenting decisions, and conflicting schedules can make co-parenting a complex and often stressful task. Unmarried mothers may also face legal and logistical hurdles when seeking financial support or custody arrangements. It is essential for single mothers to navigate these challenges while maintaining a healthy co-parenting relationship for the well-being of their children.

Societal Expectations and Pressures

Unmarried mothers face societal expectations and pressures that can be overwhelming. There is often an expectation for single mothers to be self-sufficient, to "do it all," and to prove their worth as parents. These expectations can create immense pressure and feelings of inadequacy. It is important for society to recognize and celebrate the strength and resilience of single mothers, rather than perpetuating unrealistic standards that only serve to further burden them.

Access to Resources and Support

Unmarried mothers often struggle to access essential resources and support networks. They may face difficulties in finding affordable housing, quality childcare, healthcare services, and educational opportunities for themselves and their children. Lack of access to these resources further exacerbates the challenges faced by unmarried mothers. Empowering single mothers requires providing them with comprehensive support systems that address their specific needs.

Conclusion

The challenges faced by unmarried women on the journey of unexpected motherhood are vast and complex. By acknowledging and understanding these challenges, we can empower single mothers to navigate their paths with strength and resilience. It is crucial for society to offer support, understanding, and resources that cater to the unique needs of unmarried mothers. By doing so, we can create a world where single mothers are celebrated, empowered, and given the tools to thrive in their roles as parents.

Introduction

Motherhood is a profound journey that transforms the lives of women in countless ways. While traditional notions of motherhood often revolve around a nuclear family unit, the reality is that many women embark on the journey of motherhood alone. These brave and resilient unmarried mothers face unique challenges as they navigate the complexities of raising a child without a partner. In this article, we will explore the empowering account of unmarried mothers, shedding light on their experiences, triumphs, and the lessons they can teach us all.

Choosing the Path of Unmarried Motherhood

Embracing motherhood as a single woman is a decision that requires immense courage, strength, and self-belief. Unmarried mothers often face societal judgment and stigma, which can make their journey even more challenging. However, they choose to prioritize their dreams of becoming a mother over societal expectations, challenging the status quo, and creating their own definition of family. These women show us that motherhood knows no boundaries, and the love and dedication they have for their children are unparalleled.

Overcoming Societal Stigma

Unmarried mothers frequently encounter societal prejudices and stereotypes that can make them feel isolated and judged. However, these mothers refuse to let societal stigma define their worth or their ability to provide a loving and nurturing environment for their children. They break through barriers, challenge conventional norms, and prove that single-parent households can be just as loving and successful as two-parent households. Their strength and resilience inspire us to question and redefine societal norms, paving the way for a more inclusive and compassionate society.

Building a Support Network

While unmarried mothers may not have a partner to lean on, they often establish strong support networks to help them on their journey. These networks can consist of family, friends, support groups, and other single mothers who understand the unique challenges they face. By surrounding themselves with like-minded individuals, unmarried mothers create a sense of community and find solace in knowing that they are not alone. Through their stories, we learn the importance of building a strong support system and seeking help when needed.

Nurturing Resilient Children

Unmarried mothers are determined to provide their children with the best possible upbringing, despite the challenges they face. They strive to instill in their children values of resilience, independence, and empathy, teaching them to navigate the world with grace and determination. These mothers are powerful role models, demonstrating the importance of perseverance, self-love, and embracing one's individuality. By nurturing resilient children, unmarried mothers shape the next generation and contribute to building a more inclusive and compassionate society.

Self-Care and Personal Growth

As unmarried mothers focus on raising their children, it is crucial for them to prioritize self-care and personal growth. Taking care of themselves allows them to be better caregivers, role models, and individuals. Unmarried mothers understand the importance of self-love, setting boundaries, and pursuing their own dreams and aspirations. They show us that embracing motherhood alone does not mean sacrificing personal fulfillment and happiness.

Conclusion

The stories of unmarried mothers on their journey through motherhood are a testament to the strength, resilience, and love that these remarkable women embody. By embracing motherhood alone, they challenge societal norms, break down barriers, and empower themselves and their children. Their stories inspire us to celebrate the diverse paths to motherhood and recognize the incredible strength of single mothers. By shedding light on their experiences and triumphs, we can create a more inclusive and supportive society that uplifts and empowers all mothers, regardless of their marital status. The unmarried mother's story is a story of courage, love, and the limitless possibilities of motherhood.

Chapter 4. Single Motherhood by Choice
Embracing the Journey

Introduction

Single motherhood by choice is a path that many women are courageously choosing to embark upon, defying societal norms and expectations. This intentional decision is not without its challenges, but it is a journey that can be incredibly empowering and fulfilling. In this article, we will explore the experiences of single mothers by choice, the reasons behind their decisions, the support available to them, and the joys and triumphs they encounter along the way. By shedding light on this unique journey, we aim to empower single mothers and inspire society to embrace and uplift them.

Understanding Single Motherhood by Choice

Single motherhood by choice refers to the decision made by women to become mothers without a partner. This decision is often preceded by careful consideration, reflection, and sometimes, assisted reproductive technologies. Women who choose this path are driven by a deep desire for motherhood and a strong sense of self-determination. They acknowledge that while challenges may arise, they are fully capable of providing a loving and nurturing environment for their children.

Reasons behind Choosing Single Motherhood

There are a multitude of reasons why women choose single motherhood. Some may have prioritized their careers and postponed starting a family until they felt ready, only to find themselves without a partner at a later stage in life.

Others may have experienced unfulfilling or abusive relationships, and opting for single motherhood provides an opportunity to break free from those negative dynamics. Additionally, societal shifts and changing attitudes have made single motherhood a more acceptable choice, reducing the stigma once associated with it.

Overcoming Challenges

Like any journey, single motherhood by choice has its share of challenges. Financial stability is often a concern, as women may have to navigate the complexities of raising a child on a single income. Balancing work, child-rearing, and personal well-being can also be demanding. However, single mothers by choice possess a remarkable resilience and determination. They often develop strong support networks, seek out community resources, and tap into their own inner strength to overcome these obstacles.

Building Support Networks

Recognizing the importance of support, many single mothers by choice actively seek out communities that offer understanding, encouragement, and practical assistance. Local support groups, online forums, and social media communities can provide invaluable guidance, shared experiences, and emotional support. Furthermore, these networks allow single mothers to connect with other families, forging strong bonds and creating a sense of belonging for themselves and their children.

Celebrating the Joys of Single Motherhood

Amidst the challenges, single mothers by choice also experience immeasurable joy and fulfillment. They witness their children grow and flourish under their love and guidance, and cherish the special bond they share. The journey of single motherhood fosters independence, resilience, and personal growth, allowing women to discover their own strength and capabilities. The pride and satisfaction that come with successfully navigating this path are unparalleled.

Society's Role in Empowering Single Mothers

To truly empower single mothers by choice, society must embrace and support them without judgment. Policies should be in place to provide affordable childcare, flexible work arrangements, and accessible healthcare. Employers can foster an inclusive work environment that recognizes the unique challenges faced by single mothers and provides the necessary support. Additionally, education and awareness campaigns can help dispel misconceptions and reduce the stigma surrounding single motherhood.

Conclusion

Single motherhood by choice is a journey that requires courage, resilience, and a strong sense of self. Despite the challenges, women who embark on this path find empowerment, joy, and fulfillment in their roles as mothers. By embracing and supporting single mothers, society can help create a nurturing environment that uplifts these women and their children. The stories and experiences of single mothers by choice serve as a testament to their strength and determination, inspiring others to embrace their own journeys and to celebrate the diversity of family structures in today's world.

Introduction

Co-parenting can be a challenging journey for anyone, but for single mothers, it often comes with its own unique set of difficulties. The responsibilities of raising a child alone while navigating a co-parenting relationship can be overwhelming and emotionally draining. However, with the right strategies and support, single mothers can effectively cope with the challenges that co-parenting presents. This article aims to explore the specific challenges single mothers face in co-parenting and provide empowering strategies to help them navigate this journey successfully.

Emotional Challenges

Being a single mother and co-parenting can take an emotional toll on one's well-being. Single mothers may experience a range of emotional challenges, including feelings of guilt and self-doubt. They may blame themselves for the breakdown of the relationship and question their ability to provide for their child's emotional and financial needs. Additionally, dealing with unresolved feelings of resentment and anger towards the ex-partner can make communication and collaboration difficult. Moreover, single mothers may experience loneliness and isolation due to the absence of a partner or a lack of social support.

To cope with these emotional challenges, it is crucial for single mothers to seek therapy or counseling. Professional support can help them navigate their emotions, develop coping strategies, and build resilience. Joining support groups can also provide a sense of community and support by connecting with other single mothers in similar situations. Engaging in activities that promote self-care, such as exercise, hobbies, and spending quality time with friends, can help reduce stress and improve overall well-being.

Communication and Co-Parenting Challenges

Effective communication is crucial for successful co-parenting, but it can be particularly challenging for single mothers. Differences in parenting styles can lead to conflicts and disagreements between co-parents. The lack of cooperation from the other parent can make it difficult to reach agreements, coordinate schedules, and make important decisions regarding the child's upbringing. Managing conflicts that arise between co-parents, whether from unresolved issues from the past or disagreements about parenting choices, can add to the challenges.

To cope with communication and co-parenting challenges, single mothers should focus on the child's best interests. Keeping the child's well-being at the forefront can help approach co-parenting with empathy and cooperation. Establishing clear boundaries and expectations regarding communication, visitation, and decision-making can help minimize misunderstandings. In situations where communication is strained, involving a neutral third party or a mediator can facilitate more productive discussions and resolutions.

Balancing Parenting and Self-Care

Single mothers often find it challenging to balance their responsibilities as a parent with taking care of their own needs. Neglecting self-care can lead to exhaustion, burnout, and decreased overall well-being.

To cope with the challenges of balancing parenting and self-care, single mothers should prioritize self-care. Carving out time for activities that bring them joy, relaxation, and rejuvenation is essential. Asking for help is important as well. Single mothers should seek and accept help from family, friends, or support services to share the parenting responsibilities and provide respite. Creating a support network of trusted individuals who can offer assistance, advice, or simply lend a listening ear can alleviate the sense of isolation and provide valuable support.

Navigating Legal and Financial Challenges

Single mothers may face legal and financial hurdles when it comes to co-parenting. Child support and custody issues can be complex and emotionally challenging. Single mothers may encounter difficulties in obtaining child support payments or face custody disputes that require legal intervention. Additionally, the financial strain of raising a child alone can add to the overall challenges.

To cope with the legal and financial challenges, single mothers should consult with legal professionals to seek advice and understand their rights and options. This can help navigate child support and custody issues effectively. Creating a budget and exploring available financial assistance programs, grants, or scholarships can help alleviate the financial burden. Moreover, developing financial management skills through financial literacy programs can empower single mothers to make informed decisions and secure their financial future.

Conclusion

Co-parenting as a single mother can present numerous challenges, but it is important to remember that with the right strategies and support, these challenges can be overcome. By addressing emotional well-being, improving communication, finding a balance between parenting and self-care, and navigating legal and financial hurdles, single mothers can empower themselves on their co-parenting journey. With resilience, determination, and a supportive network, single mothers can create a nurturing and stable environment for their children to thrive.

Introduction

In society's tapestry, single mothers stand as unsung heroes, weaving together the threads of love, resilience, and determination to create a better future for their children. Among these courageous women are unmarried mothers, who face a unique set of challenges as they navigate the intricate pathways of motherhood without the presence of a partner. This chapter aims to shed light on the hidden struggles that unmarried mothers often face, illuminating their silent battles and offering guidance and support to empower them on their journey.

The Stigma of Unmarried Motherhood

Unmarried mothers often find themselves confronted with social stigma, judgment, and prejudice. Society has long held a conventional view of motherhood within the confines of marriage, and those who deviate from this norm can face ostracism and discrimination. The judgmental gaze of others can lead to feelings of shame, guilt, and inadequacy, even when these women are providing their children with love and care.

Financial Hardships and Economic Insecurity

One of the most significant challenges unmarried mothers face is financial hardship. Without a partner's support, they often shoulder the entire financial burden alone. Balancing work and childcare responsibilities can be a daunting task, as many find themselves with limited employment opportunities or forced to work multiple jobs to make ends meet. The struggle to provide for their children can lead to constant stress, fear, and a sense of uncertainty about the future.

Emotional Loneliness and Isolation

Raising a child without a partner can be emotionally isolating. Unmarried mothers may lack the emotional support and companionship that a partner could provide. The absence of a co-parent to share both the joys and the challenges of parenthood can result in feelings of loneliness and overwhelm. It is crucial to recognize and address these emotional struggles by building a support network and seeking out resources that offer understanding and empathy.

Balancing Parenting and Self-Care

Unmarried mothers often find themselves caught in the delicate balancing act of being both a parent and an individual with needs and aspirations of their own. The demands of childcare, work, and household responsibilities can leave little time for self-care or personal pursuits. Neglecting one's own well-being can lead to burnout, affecting both the mother's mental and physical health. It is essential for unmarried mothers to prioritize self-care, set boundaries, and seek assistance when needed.

Co-parenting Challenges

For unmarried mothers who share custody with the child's father, navigating the complexities of co-parenting can be particularly challenging. Communication difficulties, disagreements over parenting styles, and power imbalances can strain the relationship between the parents, ultimately affecting the child's well-being. Developing effective communication strategies, seeking mediation if necessary, and focusing on the child's best interests can help unmarried mothers overcome these co-parenting hurdles.

Building a Support Network

Creating a robust support network is crucial for unmarried mothers, as it can provide the much-needed emotional, practical, and logistical support. Surrounding oneself with trusted friends, family members, and support groups can help alleviate feelings of isolation and provide a safe space to share experiences and seek advice. Community resources and organizations geared towards assisting single mothers can also offer valuable guidance and support.

Empowering Unmarried Mothers

Empowerment is vital in helping unmarried mothers overcome their silent battles and thrive on their journey. Encouraging self-belief, resilience, and self-advocacy can help them reclaim their strength and resilience. Providing access to education, job training, and financial resources can contribute to their economic stability and independence. Furthermore, destigmatizing unmarried motherhood through education and advocacy efforts can foster a more inclusive and accepting society.

Conclusion

Unmarried mothers face numerous hidden struggles in their journey of single parenthood. The societal stigma, financial hardships, emotional isolation, and co-parenting challenges can all take a toll on their well-being. However, by acknowledging these silent battles and providing support, resources, and empowerment, we can help unmarried mothers rise above these challenges and create fulfilling lives for themselves and their children. Let us stand together in solidarity with unmarried mothers, celebrating their strength and resilience as they navigate the uncharted territories of single motherhood.

Chapter 7. Thriving Against Odds
Inspiring Single Mothers' Stories

Introduction

In today's world, being a single mother comes with its own unique set of challenges. These remarkable women face the daunting task of juggling multiple responsibilities, often without the support of a partner. However, despite the adversities they encounter, single mothers around the globe have proven time and again that they are capable of not just surviving but thriving. This chapter aims to shed light on the inspiring stories of single mothers who have defied the odds, empowered themselves, and created a better future for themselves and their children.

Fictional Stories Reflecting Resilience and Determination

The stories presented in this chapter, including the names and specific details of the individuals, are fictional and created for illustrative purposes. They are not based on real people or events. However, they are inspired by the experiences and challenges faced by single mothers in general, and they aim to reflect the resilience and determination demonstrated by many single mothers in real life. The purpose of these stories is to inspire and provide examples of how single mothers can thrive against the odds, rather than to recount specific real-life narratives.

1. Overcoming Obstacles: Sarah's Journey

Sarah's story is a testament to the indomitable spirit of single mothers. After her husband left her unexpectedly, Sarah found herself in a state of shock and despair.

However, she quickly realized that she had to be strong for her two young children. With determination and resilience, she pursued higher education, despite the financial challenges. Sarah juggled multiple part-time jobs to support her family while attending night classes. Her unwavering commitment paid off when she graduated with honors and secured a job in her desired field. Sarah's story exemplifies the power of perseverance and the limitless possibilities that lie ahead for single mothers.

2. Creating Opportunities: Aisha's Tale

Aisha's journey as a single mother started with uncertainty and fear. With limited education and resources, she found it difficult to provide for her children. However, rather than succumbing to the circumstances, Aisha decided to take matters into her own hands. She explored entrepreneurial opportunities and started a small catering business from her home. Through sheer hard work and dedication, Aisha's venture grew exponentially, enabling her to hire employees and expand her services. Today, Aisha is a successful businesswoman and a source of inspiration for other single mothers who aspire to carve their own paths.

3. Embracing Support Networks: Maria's Triumph

Maria's story demonstrates the importance of building a strong support network as a single mother. When her husband passed away unexpectedly, Maria found herself grappling with grief and overwhelming responsibilities. However, she reached out to local community organizations and discovered a network of other single mothers facing similar challenges. Together, they formed a support group, sharing resources, advice, and emotional support. Through this network, Maria gained the strength and encouragement she needed to pursue her dreams. She completed her education, started a nonprofit organization, and now advocates for single mothers in her community. Maria's journey highlights the power of solidarity and the transformative impact of finding support in others who have walked a similar path.

4. Self-Care and Personal Growth: Emma's Story

Emma's story reminds us of the importance of self-care and personal growth in the lives of single mothers. After her divorce, Emma realized that she had neglected her own needs for far too long. Determined to prioritize her well-being, she started practicing mindfulness and engaging in regular exercise. Through these activities, Emma discovered a newfound sense of inner peace and resilience. She also pursued her passion for writing and began sharing her experiences as a single mother through a blog. Emma's dedication to self-care not only transformed her own life but also inspired countless other single mothers to prioritize their own happiness and personal growth.

5. Empowering Future Generations: Fatima's Legacy

Fatima's story is one of generational empowerment and resilience. As a single mother in a poverty-stricken neighborhood, Fatima faced numerous challenges in providing a better life for her children. However, she refused to let her circumstances define her children's future. Fatima emphasized the importance of education and encouraged her children to pursue their dreams relentlessly. Her daughter, now a successful lawyer, credits her mother's unwavering support as the driving force behind her achievements. Fatima's story exemplifies the profound impact a single mother can have on her children's lives, inspiring them to overcome adversity and create a brighter future.

Conclusion

The stories of Sarah, Aisha, Maria, Emma, and Fatima exemplify the resilience, strength, and determination of single mothers who have thrived against all odds. These women have defied societal expectations and overcome numerous challenges to create a better life for themselves and their children. Their stories serve as beacons of hope and inspiration for other single mothers on their own journeys. By showcasing their triumphs and highlighting the strategies they employed, we can empower single mothers around the world to embrace their own strength, tap into available resources, and create a future filled with possibilities. Together, we can foster a supportive environment that recognizes and uplifts the remarkable achievements of single mothers everywhere.

Chapter 8. Parenthood Redefined
The Joy and Challenges of Unmarried Motherhood

Introduction

Becoming a mother is a transformative experience that brings immense joy, love, and fulfillment. While the traditional concept of parenthood often revolves around marriage, the landscape of parenting has evolved, and unmarried motherhood has become a significant part of society. In this chapter, we will explore the unique journey of single mothers, celebrating the joys they experience while acknowledging the challenges they face. By redefining parenthood, these resilient women are embracing their roles as mothers, empowering themselves, and creating a better future for their children.

Embracing the Decision

Unmarried motherhood is a choice that some women make deliberately, while others may find themselves in this situation unexpectedly. Regardless of the circumstances, it is crucial to embrace this decision wholeheartedly. Single mothers can find empowerment and strength in their choice, recognizing that they are capable of providing a loving and nurturing environment for their children.

Building a Support System

One of the primary challenges faced by single mothers is the lack of a partner to share the responsibilities and joys of parenthood. However, this does not mean that they have to face the journey alone. Building a support system is essential for unmarried mothers, as it provides emotional support, practical assistance, and a sense of community.

Family, friends, support groups, and social networks can all play a significant role in offering the necessary support and guidance throughout the motherhood journey.

Nurturing Self-Care

Being a single mother requires tremendous dedication and selflessness. However, it is equally important for unmarried mothers to prioritize self-care. Taking care of oneself enables a mother to be the best version of herself, both for her own well-being and for her child. Balancing responsibilities, setting aside time for personal interests, and seeking self-care activities contribute to a healthier and happier life for single mothers.

Overcoming Societal Stigmas

Society often holds preconceived notions and stigmas surrounding unmarried motherhood. Single mothers may face judgment and discrimination, which can be disheartening and challenging to overcome. However, by redefining parenthood and demonstrating their strength, resilience, and love for their children, unmarried mothers can challenge these stereotypes and prove that their worth as parents is not determined by their marital status.

Financial Challenges and Independence

Financial stability is a significant concern for many single mothers. Without the support of a partner, they often bear the sole responsibility of providing for their children. However, it is important to note that financial challenges can be overcome through careful budgeting, seeking employment opportunities, and exploring available resources. Unmarried mothers can empower themselves by developing financial independence and resilience, ensuring a secure future for their children.

Co-Parenting and Shared Custody

In some cases, unmarried mothers may navigate co-parenting and shared custody arrangements with the child's other biological parent. These situations can bring both opportunities and challenges. Effective communication, respect, and prioritizing the child's well-being are essential for successful co-parenting relationships. Single mothers who engage in co-parenting find empowerment in actively shaping their child's life and fostering healthy relationships with both parents.

Celebrating Milestones and Bonding

Parenthood is filled with precious moments and milestones that deserve to be celebrated. Unmarried mothers have the opportunity to create unique and loving bonds with their children, cherishing every milestone and accomplishment. By being actively involved in their children's lives, single mothers can foster deep connections, provide emotional support, and create a stable and nurturing environment.

Seeking Professional Support

Unmarried motherhood can present various challenges, and it is important for single mothers to know that seeking professional support is a sign of strength, not weakness. Therapists, counselors, and parenting coaches can offer guidance, assistance, and emotional support when navigating the complexities of parenthood. Taking advantage of these resources can help unmarried mothers gain confidence and overcome challenges effectively.

Conclusion

Parenthood redefined encompasses the joy and challenges of unmarried motherhood. Single mothers are carving their paths, embracing their roles, and empowering themselves along the journey. By building support systems, practicing self-care, and challenging societal stigmas, these remarkable women are proving that marital status does not determine one's ability to be a loving and capable parent. The unique experiences, love, and dedication of unmarried mothers are shaping the future, empowering not only themselves but also their children, and creating a society that recognizes the diverse forms of parenthood.

Introduction

Becoming a single parent is a life-altering experience that often brings a unique set of challenges. However, it is also a journey that offers great freedom and the opportunity for personal growth. In this chapter, we will explore the concept of embracing independence as a single parent and delve into the various freedoms and challenges that arise along the way. By understanding and addressing these aspects, single mothers can empower themselves and embrace their role as strong, capable individuals.

Redefining Independence

Independence takes on a new meaning when one becomes a single parent. It involves self-reliance, both emotionally and financially, as well as the ability to make decisions and take responsibility for oneself and one's children. This section will discuss the process of redefining independence and the importance of cultivating a sense of self-worth and confidence.

1. Emotional Independence

Nurturing self-esteem: Building a positive self-image and recognizing personal strengths are essential for emotional well-being as a single parent.

Seeking support: Developing a network of friends, family, and support groups helps alleviate feelings of loneliness and provides a vital emotional safety net.

Managing stress: **Effective stress management techniques, such as self-care, mindfulness, and seeking therapy, contribute to emotional resilience.**

2. Financial Independence

Budgeting and financial planning: **Creating a realistic budget and understanding financial resources and expenses help single mothers gain control over their finances.**

Seeking financial support: **Exploring available resources, such as government assistance programs or child support, can help alleviate financial burdens.**

Pursuing education and career opportunities: **Enhancing education and acquiring job skills can lead to better employment prospects, increasing financial independence in the long term.**

Freedom in Decision-Making

Being a single parent means having the freedom to make choices that align with one's values and goals. This section will explore the empowering aspects of decision-making for single mothers and highlight the importance of embracing this newfound autonomy.

1. Parenting decisions

Creating a parenting philosophy: **Defining personal parenting values and principles enables single mothers to make decisions that reflect their unique circumstances.**

Encouraging open communication: **Fostering a supportive environment where children feel comfortable expressing** their needs and concerns leads to healthier decision-making.

Balancing discipline and flexibility: Striking a balance between setting boundaries and being adaptable allows single mothers to make decisions that promote their children's growth and well-being.

2. Personal choices

Self-discovery and personal growth: Embracing single parenthood as an opportunity for personal development can lead to a sense of empowerment and self-fulfillment.

Pursuing personal interests: Single mothers can explore their passions and hobbies, which not only enhances their own well-being but also sets an example for their children to follow their dreams.

Setting boundaries and prioritizing self-care: Learning to say no, establishing boundaries, and practicing self-care are vital for maintaining physical and emotional well-being.

Overcoming Challenges

While single parenthood offers freedoms, it also presents unique challenges. This section will address some common obstacles faced by single mothers and provide strategies for overcoming them.

1. Managing time and responsibilities

Establishing routines: Implementing structured routines can help single mothers manage household chores, childcare, and personal time effectively.

Seeking assistance: Enlisting the support of family members, friends, or trusted caregivers can alleviate the burden of responsibilities and create a support system.

Practicing self-compassion: Recognizing that it is impossible to do everything perfectly and allowing oneself to make mistakes promotes self-acceptance and reduces stress.

2. Coping with societal judgments

Overcoming stigma: Challenging societal stereotypes and misconceptions about single parenthood by sharing personal experiences and advocating for change.

Building a support network: Surrounding oneself with like-minded individuals who understand the challenges of single parenthood can provide validation and encouragement.

Prioritizing mental health: Seeking professional help, participating in support groups, or engaging in mindfulness practices can help single mothers cope with societal pressures.

Conclusion

Embracing independence as a single mother involves redefining personal autonomy, making empowered decisions, and overcoming challenges along the journey. By nurturing emotional and financial independence, exercising freedom in decision-making, and developing strategies to overcome obstacles, single mothers can truly empower themselves. The path of single parenthood may be challenging, but it is also an opportunity for personal growth, strength, and resilience. Embracing this independence can lead to a fulfilling and rewarding experience, both for the single mother and her children.

Chapter 10. The Untold Stories
Unmarried Mothers Breaking Stereotypes

Introduction

Motherhood is a journey filled with joy, love, and challenges. For unmarried mothers, the journey can be even more complex as they navigate societal norms, stereotypes, and stigmas. However, in recent years, there has been a paradigm shift as unmarried mothers are breaking free from societal expectations and embracing their roles as empowered individuals and mothers. In this chapter, we will explore the untold stories of unmarried mothers who have defied stereotypes, overcome obstacles, and emerged as strong, resilient women on their journey of empowerment.

Challenging the Stigma

Unmarried mothers have long faced societal stigma and judgment. They have been subjected to labels and stereotypes that undermine their abilities as mothers. However, these untold stories reveal a different reality. They showcase the strength and determination of unmarried mothers who refuse to let societal expectations define them. They challenge the stigma by demonstrating their unwavering love, dedication, and commitment to their children.

Building Support Networks

One crucial aspect of empowering unmarried mothers is the creation of support networks. These networks play a pivotal role in breaking the isolation that many unmarried mothers experience. These untold stories shed light on the importance of finding supportive communities, whether it be through online platforms, local support groups, or organizations that cater specifically to the needs of unmarried mothers. These networks provide emotional support, guidance, and resources, enabling unmarried mothers to overcome challenges and thrive.

Pursuing Education and Career Goals

Another stereotype that unmarried mothers often face is the assumption that their educational and career aspirations must be put on hold. However, these untold stories reveal a different narrative. They showcase unmarried mothers who refuse to let their circumstances limit their potential. Through determination and resilience, they pursue higher education, skill development, and career opportunities. By doing so, they not only secure a better future for themselves but also set a positive example for their children, instilling the value of education and hard work.

Redefining Relationships

Unmarried mothers often face challenges in their relationships, whether it be with the biological father of their child, their own families, or potential partners. However, these untold stories highlight the strength of unmarried mothers in redefining relationships on their own terms. They show how unmarried mothers can establish healthy co-parenting arrangements, foster positive connections with their families, and navigate the complexities of dating and relationships. By doing so, they demonstrate that unmarried motherhood does not equate to a lack of love or support.

Embracing Self-Care and Well-being

The journey of empowerment for unmarried mothers involves prioritizing self-care and well-being. These untold stories emphasize the importance of unmarried mothers taking care of themselves physically, emotionally, and mentally. They demonstrate that self-care is not a luxury but a necessity, enabling unmarried mothers to be the best version of themselves for their children. From seeking therapy and practicing mindfulness to engaging in hobbies and pursuing personal passions, these stories exemplify the power of self-love and self-care.

Overcoming Financial Challenges

Financial stability is a significant concern for many unmarried mothers. These untold stories shed light on the resourcefulness and resilience of unmarried mothers in overcoming financial challenges. From seeking employment and entrepreneurship opportunities to accessing financial assistance programs and scholarships, these stories demonstrate that financial independence is attainable for unmarried mothers. They inspire other unmarried mothers to explore avenues for economic empowerment and overcome the limitations imposed by societal expectations.

Conclusion

The untold stories of unmarried mothers breaking stereotypes are a testament to the strength, resilience, and determination of these women. Through their unwavering love for their children and their refusal to let societal norms define them, they have redefined what it means to be an unmarried mother. These stories inspire and empower other unmarried mothers, showing them that they are not alone and that they have the ability to overcome any obstacle. By sharing these untold stories, we hope to shatter stereotypes and create a more inclusive and supportive society that recognizes and celebrates the power of unmarried mothers on their journey of empowerment.

Introduction

Life has a way of throwing unexpected challenges our way, and for many single mothers, the loss of a spouse can be one of the most devastating experiences. Suddenly finding themselves navigating the world alone, single mothers who have become widows often face a unique set of emotional, financial, and practical challenges. However, within the pain and grief lies an opportunity for growth, resilience, and the discovery of a new path towards hope and healing. In this chapter, we will explore the journey of the widow and discuss empowering strategies to find hope and healing amidst adversity.

Embracing Grief and Loss

1. Acknowledging and Expressing Emotions

Grief is a natural response to loss, and it is important for single mothers to acknowledge and honor their emotions. From anger and sadness to confusion and guilt, the grieving process can be complex and unpredictable. By allowing themselves to feel and express these emotions, single mothers can begin to navigate their grief and move towards healing.

2. Seeking Support Systems

During times of grief, it is crucial for single mothers to lean on their support systems. Friends, family, and support groups can provide a safe space for expression, understanding, and compassion. Surrounding oneself with individuals who empathize and offer practical assistance can help alleviate the burden of grief and provide a sense of comfort and hope.

Redefining Identity and Purpose

1. Rediscovering Self

The loss of a spouse often prompts single mothers to reassess their identity and sense of self. It is essential to embark on a journey of self-discovery, recognizing that they are more than just a widow. Exploring interests, talents, and passions can be a catalyst for personal growth and the development of a new identity.

2. Realigning Priorities

Becoming a single mother also necessitates a reevaluation of priorities. Widows must determine what matters most to them and their children, and make conscious choices that align with their values. This process involves setting new goals and creating a roadmap for the future, instilling a sense of purpose and direction.

Navigating Financial Challenges

1. Assessing Financial Resources

The loss of a spouse often brings financial uncertainty, and single mothers must face the realities of their new financial situation. It is crucial to take stock of available resources, including life insurance, savings, and support networks. Seeking professional financial advice can provide guidance on budgeting, investment strategies, and long-term planning.

To alleviate financial burdens, single mothers can explore opportunities to increase their income and secure their financial future. This may involve pursuing higher education or vocational training, starting a small business, or seeking employment that offers flexibility and stability. Empowering oneself financially can provide a sense of independence and security.

Building a Supportive Network

1. Cultivating Relationships

Creating a strong support network is vital for single mothers on their journey of healing. Building relationships with other single mothers, joining community groups, or engaging in activities that align with personal interests can foster connections and provide a sense of belonging. Sharing experiences, advice, and encouragement can make the path towards healing less lonely.

2. Seeking Professional Help

While the support of loved ones is invaluable, professional guidance can also play a significant role in the healing process. Therapists, counselors, and support groups specifically tailored for widows can offer a safe space to process emotions, gain insights, and learn coping strategies. Seeking professional help is a sign of strength and self-care.

Embracing Hope and Moving Forward

1. Cultivating Resilience

Resilience is the ability to bounce back from adversity, and single mothers must cultivate this trait to overcome the challenges they face. Developing a positive mindset, practicing self-care, and embracing a growth-oriented perspective can strengthen resilience and provide the inner strength needed to move forward.

2. Embracing New Beginnings

Finding hope after loss involves embracing new beginnings. Single mothers can create new traditions, explore new hobbies, and engage in activities that bring joy and fulfillment. By embracing the possibilities that lie ahead, widows can find hope, healing, and a renewed sense of purpose.

Conclusion

The path of a widow can be arduous, but it is not devoid of hope and healing. By acknowledging and expressing emotions, embracing personal growth, navigating financial challenges, building a supportive network, and cultivating resilience, single mothers can find solace, strength, and a renewed sense of purpose. As they embark on this journey, it is important for widows to remember that they are not alone. With time, support, and self-compassion, they can empower themselves, find hope in the face of adversity, and build a brighter future for themselves and their children.

Introduction

Becoming a widow is a deeply painful and life-altering experience that no one is ever fully prepared for. The loss of a spouse not only shatters dreams and stability but also leaves a void that seems impossible to fill. For single mothers, the challenges of widowhood are further compounded as they navigate the complexities of grief while taking on the responsibilities of raising children alone. However, amidst the overwhelming sorrow and uncertainty, there is hope. This chapter explores the journey of rebuilding life as a widow, empowering single mothers to find strength, discover their identity, and embrace new beginnings.

Acknowledging and Navigating Grief

The first step towards rebuilding life after losing a spouse is acknowledging and allowing oneself to grieve. Grief is a complex and personal journey that varies from person to person. Single mothers need to understand that it is okay to experience a wide range of emotions, including anger, sadness, guilt, and confusion. They should seek support from family, friends, or even professional counselors who can provide a safe space for them to express their feelings and cope with the loss. It is crucial to remember that healing takes time, and everyone moves through grief at their own pace.

Embracing Self-Care

During this difficult time, it is crucial for single mothers to prioritize self-care. Widowhood often brings a multitude of responsibilities, both emotionally and practically. However, neglecting self-care can lead to burnout and hinder the healing process. Single mothers should make time for activities that bring them joy and provide an outlet for stress. This could include exercise, meditation, hobbies, or connecting with supportive social networks. By taking care of themselves, single mothers can regain their strength and better support their children in the process.

Building a Support System

No one should have to face widowhood alone. Creating a strong support system is vital for single mothers as they rebuild their lives. Friends, family, and support groups can offer emotional support, practical assistance, and a sense of belonging. It is essential to reach out and ask for help when needed, as people are often willing to provide assistance but may not know how to offer it. Connecting with other widows can be particularly valuable, as they can provide empathy and understanding based on their own experiences.

Redefining Identity

Losing a spouse often forces single mothers to reevaluate their identity and role in life. It is crucial to understand that widowhood does not define a person entirely. Single mothers should take the time to reflect on their passions, strengths, and goals. This can involve rediscovering old hobbies, pursuing new interests, or even considering career advancements. By focusing on personal growth, single mothers can gradually develop a renewed sense of self and purpose, allowing them to navigate the challenges of single parenting more effectively.

Nurturing Parent-Child Relationships

As a widow, the responsibility of raising children falls solely on the single mother. Strengthening the parent-child relationship is crucial for both emotional support and maintaining a sense of stability. Open and honest communication helps children process their own grief and build resilience. Setting aside quality time for shared activities and fostering a safe environment for expressing emotions can strengthen the bonds within the family unit. Single mothers should also be mindful of balancing the role of both parents, providing love, discipline, and guidance, while allowing space for the child to mourn their loss in their own way.

Financial Planning and Independence

Widowhood often brings about financial challenges and uncertainties. Single mothers must take steps to secure their financial future and gain independence. This may involve reviewing and adjusting budgets, exploring job opportunities or career development, and seeking financial advice or assistance. Developing a solid financial plan provides a sense of stability and empowers single mothers to take control of their lives, both for themselves and their children.

Embracing New Beginnings

Rebuilding life as a widow involves embracing new beginnings. It is important to recognize that moving forward does not mean forgetting or dishonoring the past. Single mothers should allow themselves to dream and set new goals for the future. This could include pursuing education, exploring new relationships, or finding new avenues for personal and professional growth. Embracing new experiences with an open heart can bring about unexpected joy and help in the healing process.

Conclusion

Rebuilding life as a widow is a journey of strength, resilience, and self-discovery. While the pain of loss never truly disappears, it is possible for single mothers to rebuild a fulfilling and meaningful life. By acknowledging grief, prioritizing self-care, building a support system, redefining identity, nurturing parent-child relationships, ensuring financial independence, and embracing new beginnings, single mothers can find empowerment on their journey as widows. Remember, the path forward may not be easy, but it is one that is filled with hope and the potential for a bright future.

Chapter 13. Widows and Self-Discovery
Finding Identity Beyond Loss

Introduction

Losing a spouse is one of the most devastating experiences a person can go through, and for single mothers who find themselves widowed, the journey becomes even more challenging. The loss of a partner not only brings emotional turmoil but also forces them to navigate a new reality of single parenthood. However, amidst the pain and grief, there lies an opportunity for self-discovery and finding a new identity beyond the loss. In this chapter, we will explore the journey of widows as they embark on a path of self-discovery, reclaim their identities, and empower themselves as single mothers.

Embracing the Grief Process

The grieving process is a necessary part of healing after the loss of a spouse. Widows often find themselves overwhelmed with emotions, ranging from shock and denial to anger, sadness, and acceptance. It is crucial for widows to allow themselves to fully experience and process these emotions. Through various therapeutic techniques such as counseling, support groups, and self-reflection, widows can begin to navigate their grief and gradually find solace in their journey.

Rebuilding Identity

When a widow loses her spouse, she often finds herself questioning her identity. For years, her role may have been defined by her marriage and motherhood, but with the loss, she must redefine herself. It is essential for widows to recognize that they are more than just a wife or mother. Engaging in activities they are passionate about, pursuing hobbies, and discovering new interests can help widows rebuild their sense of self. By exploring their talents and strengths, widows can discover their individual identities and regain their confidence.

Nurturing Emotional and Mental Well-being

Self-care becomes imperative for widows on their journey of self-discovery. Prioritizing emotional and mental well-being allows them to heal and move forward. Engaging in practices such as meditation, journaling, exercise, and seeking therapy can provide widows with the tools they need to process their emotions, develop resilience, and cultivate a positive mindset. By nurturing their well-being, widows can emerge stronger and more equipped to handle the challenges of single motherhood.

Building a Support Network

Navigating the world as a single mother can be isolating, but building a strong support network can make all the difference. Widows should seek out individuals who can provide emotional support, practical advice, and companionship. This network can include family members, friends, support groups, or even online communities specifically tailored to widows. By surrounding themselves with compassionate and understanding individuals, widows can find solace in knowing they are not alone in their journey.

Redefining Relationships

Losing a spouse often impacts other relationships in a widow's life, including friendships and familial ties. Some friendships may fade away due to a lack of understanding or discomfort with the widow's grief. However, this loss can also provide an opportunity to cultivate new relationships and deepen existing ones with individuals who are supportive and empathetic. Additionally, widows must establish healthy boundaries with their extended families and create a network of support for their children.

Embracing Financial Independence

Financial concerns often arise when a widow loses her spouse, making it crucial to focus on financial empowerment. Widows should seek guidance from financial professionals to understand their options, manage their finances, and plan for the future. Learning about budgeting, investments, and insurance can provide widows with the knowledge and confidence to make sound financial decisions. By embracing financial independence, widows can secure their own futures and provide for their families.

Embracing Motherhood as a Strength

Single motherhood can be seen as a challenge, but it is also a unique strength. Widows should recognize and embrace the resilience, strength, and love they possess as they navigate the dual roles of mother and father. By fostering a supportive and nurturing environment, widows can raise children who understand the importance of resilience, empathy, and independence.

Reimagining the Future

As widows embark on their journey of self-discovery, they must also reimagine their futures. This involves setting new goals, dreaming new dreams, and envisioning a life filled with joy and purpose. By creating a vision for themselves and their families, widows can find the motivation to overcome obstacles and pursue new opportunities. With a newfound sense of identity and resilience, widows can shape their futures in a way that honors their past while embracing the possibilities that lie ahead.

Conclusion

The journey of widows is a testament to the human spirit's resilience and capacity for growth. By embracing the grief process, rebuilding their identities, nurturing their emotional well-being, building support networks, embracing financial independence, and reimagining their futures, widows can embark on a path of self-discovery and empowerment. Through their journey, they not only find their own identities but also become role models for their children and inspire others with their strength and determination. Widows have the power to create a life filled with purpose, love, and joy beyond their loss, empowering themselves and other single mothers on their journey.

Introduction

Losing a spouse is one of the most devastating experiences a person can go through. The journey of widowhood brings with it a myriad of challenges, and for single mothers, the emotional toll can be even more profound. The loss of a partner not only leaves a void in their lives but also affects their children and the overall family dynamics. However, amidst the grief and pain, there is hope for healing and rebuilding emotional well-being. In this chapter, we will explore the process of healing after becoming a widow and discuss practical strategies for empowering single mothers on their journey towards emotional well-being.

Understanding Grief and Loss

The first step towards healing is acknowledging and understanding the grief that accompanies the loss of a spouse. Grief is a natural response to loss, and it manifests differently for each person. It is essential to give yourself permission to grieve and allow the emotions to surface. The grieving process is not linear and may involve a range of emotions such as sadness, anger, guilt, and even relief. Recognize that these emotions are normal and part of the healing journey.

Seeking Support

One of the most critical aspects of healing as a widow is seeking and accepting support. Often, single mothers try to shoulder the entire burden on their own, fearing that asking for help might be seen as a sign of weakness. However, reaching out to friends, family, and support groups can provide invaluable support during this challenging time. Sharing your feelings and experiences with others who have gone through similar situations can be incredibly healing. Additionally, seeking professional help from therapists or grief counselors can offer guidance and tools to navigate the emotional challenges of widowhood.

Processing Emotions

Grief and loss can be overwhelming, making it essential to find healthy ways to process and express emotions. Journaling, talking to a trusted friend, or joining a support group can provide a safe space to share your feelings. Engaging in activities that promote self-expression, such as art, music, or writing, can also be therapeutic. Furthermore, practicing self-compassion and allowing yourself to experience the full range of emotions without judgment is crucial for emotional healing.

Rebuilding Identity

The loss of a spouse often causes a significant shift in one's identity. As a widow and a single mother, you may find yourself redefining who you are and what your life looks like. Embracing this process of self-discovery can be empowering. Take the time to reconnect with your passions, hobbies, and personal goals. Explore new interests and opportunities that align with your values and desires. Remember, your identity extends beyond your role as a wife or a mother, and reclaiming your individuality is an integral part of healing and emotional well-being.

Nurturing Self-Care

Caring for yourself is not a luxury but a necessity, especially during the healing process. As a single mother, it is easy to neglect self-care while tending to the needs of your children. However, prioritizing your well-being is crucial for rebuilding emotional resilience. Set aside time for activities that bring you joy and relaxation, such as exercise, meditation, or spending time in nature. Prioritize good nutrition and adequate sleep to support your physical and emotional health. Remember, by taking care of yourself, you are also setting a positive example for your children.

Parenting Through Grief

The loss of a parent profoundly impacts children, and as a single mother, you play a crucial role in helping them navigate their own grief. It is essential to create a safe environment where children feel comfortable expressing their emotions and asking questions. Encourage open communication and validate their feelings. Seek age-appropriate resources and support to help them understand and process their emotions effectively. Remember, you do not have to have all the answers, and seeking professional guidance can be beneficial for both you and your children.

Building a Support Network

Creating a strong support network is vital for single mothers who have lost their spouse. Surround yourself with individuals who provide emotional support, practical assistance, and positive influences. Seek out other single mothers who can relate to your experiences and share the journey with you. Engaging in community activities, support groups, or online forums can help expand your network and offer a sense of belonging.

Conclusion

The journey of healing after becoming a widow is not an easy one, but it is possible to rebuild emotional well-being and find renewed purpose and joy in life. By acknowledging and processing grief, seeking support, nurturing self-care, and empowering yourself as a single mother, you can create a foundation for healing and emotional resilience. Remember, you are not alone on this journey, and with time and self-compassion, you can heal your heart and empower yourself and your children to thrive.

Introduction

The loss of a spouse is an incredibly difficult and life-altering experience, especially for single mothers who are suddenly faced with the challenges of raising children on their own. Widows often find themselves grappling with grief, financial instability, and a sense of isolation. However, within the widowed community, there can be a growing movement of support and empowerment known as "*Widows United*." This chapter explores the various ways in which this support network helps widows navigate their journey, providing them with the tools and resources they need to rebuild their lives and find strength in their newfound roles as single mothers.

The Importance of Support Networks

Grief and loss can be overwhelming, but connecting with others who have experienced similar circumstances can offer immense comfort and support. Widows United recognizes the power of solidarity and creates a safe space where widows can share their stories, express their emotions, and find solace in knowing they are not alone. The network can provide both online platforms and local support groups, allowing widows to connect with others who understand their unique challenges.

Emotional Healing and Empowerment

Rebuilding a life after the loss of a spouse requires not only emotional healing but also empowerment. Widows United offers a range of resources to help widows navigate the grieving process and find strength within themselves. These resources include grief counseling, therapy services, mindfulness exercises, and self-care practices. By addressing the emotional needs of widows, the network empowers them to take control of their healing journey and embrace their newfound identity as single mothers.

Financial Guidance and Stability

One of the most significant concerns for many widows is financial stability. Losing a spouse often means a loss of income, and single mothers may find themselves struggling to make ends meet. Widows United collaborates with financial experts and organizations to provide widows with practical guidance on managing finances, creating budgets, and accessing resources such as government assistance programs and scholarships. By equipping widows with the necessary financial knowledge and tools, the network empowers them to regain control of their economic well-being.

Parenting Support and Mentorship

Raising children as a single parent can be challenging, and widows often face additional obstacles as they navigate their parenting journey alone. Widows United recognizes the need for parenting support and mentorship and facilitates connections between widows at different stages of their parenting journey. The network offers mentorship programs where experienced widows provide guidance, share their insights, and offer practical tips on coping with the demands of single parenting. These mentorship relationships not only provide valuable support but also foster a sense of community and intergenerational bonding.

Education and Skill Development

Education and skill development are crucial for widows seeking to rebuild their lives and secure better opportunities for themselves and their children. Widows United partners with educational institutions, vocational training centers, and online learning platforms to provide widows with access to educational resources. This includes scholarships, vocational training programs, and online courses tailored to their specific needs and interests. By empowering widows through education, the network helps them develop new skills, increase their employability, and expand their horizons.

Advocacy and Social Change

Widows United is not just a support network; it is also a platform for advocacy and social change. The network actively works to raise awareness about the challenges faced by widows, advocating for policies that address their specific needs. Widows United engages in community outreach, collaborates with policymakers, and partners with other organizations to challenge social stigmas, promote inclusivity, and create a supportive environment for widows and their children.

Conclusion

Widows United can be a powerful support network that empowers single mothers who have experienced the loss of a spouse. By providing emotional healing, financial guidance, parenting support, education, and advocacy, the network equips widows with the tools and resources necessary to rebuild their lives and find strength in their new roles as single parents. Through solidarity and empowerment, Widows United creates a community where widows can find support, connection, and the belief that they are not alone on their journey. Together, these widows are united in their resilience and determination to create a bright future for themselves and their children.

Chapter 16. The Resilient Widow
Overcoming Adversity and Embracing Life

Introduction

The journey of a single mother can be incredibly challenging, and for a widow, it can be even more daunting. Losing a spouse is a devastating experience that shakes the foundation of one's life. However, within the depths of grief and adversity lies the potential for remarkable strength and resilience. In this chapter, we will explore the story of the resilient widow who, despite facing unimaginable loss, finds the courage to overcome adversity and embrace life once again. Through her inspiring journey, we will discover the power of resilience and the strategies she employs to empower herself and her children.

Embracing Grief and Healing

1. The weight of loss

Losing a spouse is a life-altering event that leaves a widow grappling with intense grief and a sense of emptiness. Acknowledging the weight of loss and allowing oneself to grieve is an essential step in the healing process.

2. The power of community

A resilient widow understands the importance of surrounding herself with a supportive community. From family and friends to support groups and counselors, she seeks solace in the company of others who understand her pain and can provide a compassionate ear.

3. Self-care and healing

Self-care becomes a vital aspect of a widow's journey towards healing. Engaging in activities that promote physical, emotional, and mental well-being allows her to process her grief and regain her strength.

Redefining Identity and Purpose

1. Discovering personal strengths

The loss of a spouse often prompts a widow to redefine her identity and discover her personal strengths. Through self-reflection and self-discovery, she uncovers hidden talents, passions, and ambitions that fuel her journey towards empowerment.

2. Setting new goals

A resilient widow embraces the opportunity to set new goals and aspirations for herself and her children. By envisioning a future filled with purpose and meaning, she creates a roadmap for success and finds the motivation to overcome any obstacles that come her way.

3. Inspiring her children

A widow's resilience serves as a powerful example to her children. By witnessing their mother's determination to rebuild their lives, they learn the value of perseverance, adaptability, and resilience, which will shape their own journeys in the face of adversity.

Financial Independence and Stability

1. Navigating financial challenges

A widow often faces significant financial challenges in the aftermath of losing a spouse. However, a resilient widow takes proactive steps to gain financial independence, whether it's through seeking employment, starting a business, or exploring available resources and support systems.

2. Financial planning and budgeting

Taking charge of her financial future, a resilient widow learns the importance of effective financial planning and budgeting. By setting financial goals, creating a budget, and making wise financial decisions, she establishes a stable foundation for herself and her children.

3. Building a support network

Navigating financial challenges alone can be overwhelming. A resilient widow seeks out resources and support networks that can provide guidance and assistance, such as financial advisors, community organizations, and government programs.

Embracing Life and New Beginnings

1. Cultivating a positive mindset

A resilient widow understands the power of a positive mindset in overcoming adversity. By reframing her perspective and focusing on gratitude, she cultivates resilience and finds the strength to embrace life's new beginnings.

To fully embrace life and experience personal growth, a widow must step out of her comfort zone. Whether it's pursuing new interests, taking on new challenges, or exploring new relationships, embracing change becomes a catalyst for empowerment.

3. Finding joy and purpose

Through her resilience, a widow discovers the importance of finding joy and purpose in everyday life. By engaging in activities that bring her happiness and align with her values, she creates a life filled with meaning and fulfillment for herself and her children.

Conclusion

The journey of a resilient widow is a testament to the power of the human spirit. Through her ability to overcome adversity and embrace life, she becomes an inspiration to other single mothers facing similar challenges. By embracing grief, redefining her identity, attaining financial independence, and embracing new beginnings, she transforms her story into one of triumph. The resilient widow teaches us that, no matter the circumstances, it is possible to rise above adversity and create a life of empowerment, resilience, and happiness.

Introduction

Becoming a single mother is often a life-altering experience that brings forth a whirlwind of emotions, challenges, and uncertainties. While the journey may be daunting, it also offers an opportunity for personal growth, resilience, and empowerment. In this article, we will explore the various aspects of life as a single mother and provide valuable insights and guidance for navigating this transformative journey.

Embracing Change and Self-Discovery

When transitioning into the role of a single mother, it is crucial to embrace change and embark on a journey of self-discovery. This involves understanding and accepting the new dynamics of your life, acknowledging your strengths, and finding your own identity outside of the traditional family structure. Take the time to reconnect with your passions, explore new interests, and invest in self-care. By nurturing yourself, you create a strong foundation for both you and your children.

Building a Support Network

One of the most valuable assets for single mothers is a strong support network. Seek out family members, friends, and community resources that can provide emotional support, practical assistance, and guidance. Join local support groups, single-parent organizations, or online communities where you can connect with other single mothers facing similar challenges. Sharing experiences and insights can provide a sense of belonging and offer a wealth of knowledge and advice.

Prioritizing Financial Stability

Financial stability is a common concern for single mothers, as they bear the sole responsibility of supporting their families. Take charge of your financial situation by creating a budget, identifying potential income sources, and exploring career opportunities or educational programs that can enhance your earning potential. Seek professional advice on financial planning, investment options, and government assistance programs that can provide a safety net during challenging times.

Nurturing Positive Co-Parenting Relationships

If you share custody or have a co-parenting arrangement, nurturing a positive relationship with your child's other parent is vital. Effective communication, mutual respect, and cooperation can create a harmonious environment for your child's upbringing. Focus on the best interests of your child, establish clear boundaries, and maintain open lines of communication. By working together, you can provide your child with the stability and support they need.

Creating a Healthy Routine

Establishing a structured and healthy routine is essential for both you and your children. Structure provides stability and a sense of security, especially during times of transition. Set regular bedtimes, plan nutritious meals, and ensure your children have a designated study and play area. Encourage open communication and involve your children in decision-making processes, allowing them to have a sense of control and responsibility.

Cultivating Emotional Well-being

As a single mother, it's crucial to prioritize your emotional well-being and that of your children. Encourage open dialogue about feelings, thoughts, and concerns. Create a safe space where your children feel comfortable expressing themselves without judgment. Seek professional help if needed, such as therapy or counseling services, to address any emotional or mental health challenges that may arise.

Balancing Parenting and Self-Care

Finding a balance between being a dedicated parent and taking care of yourself is crucial for your overall well-being. It's essential to carve out time for self-care activities, whether it's exercising, pursuing hobbies, or simply enjoying moments of solitude. Remember that taking care of yourself allows you to show up as the best version of yourself for your children.

Embracing Personal Growth and Empowerment

Single motherhood presents an opportunity for personal growth and empowerment. Embrace the challenges as stepping stones towards a brighter future. Set goals for yourself and celebrate milestones, no matter how small. Continuously seek knowledge and personal development through books, courses, or workshops that align with your interests or career aspirations. By investing in your personal growth, you demonstrate resilience and inspire your children to do the same.

Conclusion

Navigating life as a single mother can be both challenging and rewarding. By embracing change, building a support network, prioritizing financial stability, nurturing positive co-parenting relationships, creating a healthy routine, cultivating emotional well-being, balancing parenting and self-care, and embracing personal growth, you can embark on a journey of empowerment and find fulfillment in both your role as a mother and as an individual. Remember, you are capable, strong, and deserving of a bright future. You have the power to create a new beginning for yourself and your children.

Introduction

Motherhood is a remarkable journey filled with love, joy, and challenges. For unmarried mothers, the path can be even more demanding as they face societal stereotypes, judgments, and limited support. However, it is crucial to remember that being an unmarried mother does not define a woman's ability to achieve success and create a fulfilling life for herself and her child. In this article, we will explore the remarkable experiences of unmarried mothers who have broken barriers, shattered stereotypes, and achieved remarkable success, proving that motherhood and personal accomplishments can indeed go hand in hand.

Redefining Success as an Unmarried Mother

The first step towards achieving success as an unmarried mother is redefining the concept of success itself. Society often measures success in terms of traditional norms, such as marriage, financial stability, and career accomplishments. However, for unmarried mothers, success can be more nuanced and personal. It can mean raising a happy and healthy child, pursuing education or career goals, or simply finding inner strength and resilience to navigate through life's challenges.

Education: Empowering Single Mothers

Education is a powerful tool that empowers single mothers to break the cycle of poverty and attain a better future for themselves and their children. Pursuing education not only expands their knowledge and skills but also opens doors to new opportunities. Many unmarried mothers have returned to school, obtaining degrees or vocational training, defying expectations and proving their determination to create a brighter future for their families.

Building Support Networks

The journey of an unmarried mother can be challenging, but building a strong support network can make a significant difference. Community organizations, support groups, and online platforms have emerged as crucial lifelines for unmarried mothers, providing emotional support, practical advice, and connections to resources. These networks foster a sense of belonging, diminish isolation, and help unmarried mothers navigate the ups and downs of motherhood with strength and resilience.

Financial Independence: Securing a Bright Future

Financial stability is vital for unmarried mothers to provide for their children's needs and secure a bright future. Single mothers have demonstrated immense resourcefulness and resilience in overcoming financial challenges. Some have established successful businesses, while others have pursued flexible job opportunities or sought higher-paying careers through further education. By leveraging their skills, determination, and support networks, unmarried mothers have proven that financial independence is attainable, irrespective of their marital status.

Overcoming Stigma and Stereotypes

Unmarried mothers often face societal stigma and stereotypes that can hinder their personal growth and success. They are unfairly judged and labeled, adding additional emotional and psychological burdens to their already demanding lives. However, many unmarried mothers have defied these stereotypes by embracing their journey, prioritizing their well-being, and focusing on their goals. Through self-acceptance, resilience, and surrounding themselves with positive influences, they have shattered societal expectations and emerged as role models for other unmarried mothers.

Nurturing Relationships and Self-Care

Unmarried mothers face unique challenges when it comes to nurturing relationships and practicing self-care. Balancing the responsibilities of motherhood with personal needs can be overwhelming, but it is crucial for their overall well-being and success. Many unmarried mothers have discovered the importance of self-care, setting boundaries, and seeking emotional support to maintain healthy relationships with their children and themselves. By prioritizing their mental, emotional, and physical health, they can thrive and create a loving and nurturing environment for their families.

Conclusion

The journey of an unmarried mother is a testament to the strength, resilience, and determination of women who navigate the challenges of motherhood without the traditional societal support. These women break barriers, redefine success, and prove that they are capable of achieving remarkable things in their personal and professional lives. By embracing their unique journey, building support networks, pursuing education, and prioritizing self-care, unmarried mothers are not only empowering themselves but also inspiring future generations of single mothers. Their stories are a testament to the power of determination, love, and the indomitable spirit of motherhood.

Chapter 19. Single Moms and Finances
Overcoming Economic Challenges

Introduction

In today's society, single mothers face a multitude of challenges, and one of the most significant is managing their finances. Juggling the responsibilities of parenting, household management, and employment can be overwhelming, leaving little time and energy for financial planning. However, by understanding the unique economic challenges faced by single moms and implementing effective strategies, they can regain control over their financial lives and achieve stability. This article aims to empower single mothers on their journey by providing insights and practical tips to overcome economic challenges, create a solid financial foundation, and secure a brighter future for themselves and their children.

Understanding the Economic Challenges

Single mothers often face numerous economic challenges that can impede their financial well-being. Factors such as limited income, lack of support, and the need to balance work and family commitments create a complex financial landscape. Many single moms struggle with low-wage jobs, insufficient child support, and the absence of a second income to rely on. Consequently, they may find it challenging to cover basic expenses, save for emergencies, or invest in their and their children's futures.

Creating a Budget and Managing Expenses

Creating a budget is a crucial step for single mothers in regaining control of their finances. It helps them understand their income, track their expenses, and identify areas where they can cut costs. When budgeting, single moms should prioritize essential expenses like housing, utilities, food, and healthcare. They should also consider expenses related to childcare, education, and savings. Identifying discretionary expenses and finding ways to reduce or eliminate them can free up additional funds.

Exploring Available Support and Resources

Single mothers should explore available support and resources in their communities and beyond. Many organizations and government programs offer assistance with housing, childcare, education, job training, and financial counseling. Researching and connecting with these resources can provide valuable guidance and opportunities to improve financial stability. Additionally, single mothers can reach out to support groups and networks specifically designed for single parents, where they can find emotional support, share experiences, and exchange financial tips.

Building an Emergency Fund

Creating an emergency fund is crucial for single mothers to cope with unexpected expenses or financial setbacks. Even small monthly contributions can gradually build a safety net, providing peace of mind during challenging times. Single moms can start by automating small deposits into a separate savings account or exploring micro-saving apps that round up purchases and save the spare change. Having an emergency fund safeguards against relying on credit cards or high-interest loans, reducing the risk of falling into debt.

Increasing Income Potential

Single mothers can take proactive steps to increase their income potential and secure a more stable financial future. Pursuing higher education, vocational training, or certifications can open doors to better-paying jobs or career advancement. Exploring work-from-home or flexible job opportunities can provide a better work-life balance, minimizing childcare expenses. Additionally, single mothers can consider side hustles or freelance work to supplement their income.

Investing in the Future

Investing in the future is vital for single mothers to secure their financial well-being and provide for their children's future. Creating a retirement savings plan and contributing regularly can ensure a comfortable retirement. Additionally, exploring options like college savings plans or education funds for their children demonstrates a commitment to their long-term success.

Conclusion

While the economic challenges faced by single mothers are significant, they can be overcome with determination, knowledge, and strategic planning. By understanding their financial situation, creating a budget, accessing available support and resources, building an emergency fund, increasing their income potential, and investing in the future, single mothers can regain control over their finances.

Chapter 20. The Strength of Sisterhood
Building a Community of Single Mothers

Introduction

Becoming a single mother is an extraordinary journey filled with unique challenges and triumphs. It requires immense strength, resilience, and determination to navigate the complexities of raising children alone. However, in the face of adversity, the power of sisterhood emerges as an invaluable resource. By fostering a community of single mothers, we can create a supportive network that empowers these women on their journey of parenthood. In this article, we will explore the strength of sisterhood and its transformative impact on the lives of single mothers.

Understanding the Challenges Faced by Single Mothers

Single motherhood comes with its fair share of challenges. From financial constraints to emotional stress, these women often find themselves shouldering multiple responsibilities. They face societal stigmas, judgments, and the pressure to be both mother and father figures for their children. It is essential to acknowledge these challenges and the immense strength required to overcome them.

The Power of Connection

One of the greatest gifts of sisterhood is the power of connection. By fostering a community of single mothers, we create a space where these women can come together, share their experiences, and support one another. The bond formed within this community offers solace, understanding, and encouragement. Through shared stories and empathy, single mothers realize that they are not alone in their struggles, providing them with a renewed sense of hope and resilience.

Empowering Through Shared Knowledge

Within a community of single mothers, knowledge becomes a valuable currency. Each woman brings her unique experiences, wisdom, and expertise to the table. By sharing practical advice, resources, and strategies, these women empower one another to overcome obstacles and build a better future for themselves and their children. Whether it's tips on managing finances, finding reliable childcare, or balancing work and family life, the collective knowledge within the community becomes a catalyst for growth and progress.

Breaking the Isolation

Single motherhood can often be isolating, leading to feelings of loneliness and despair. By establishing a community of support, we break the cycle of isolation. Through regular gatherings, meetups, and online platforms, single mothers can connect with like-minded individuals who understand their struggles intimately. This sense of belonging helps combat feelings of isolation, fostering a support system that uplifts and encourages every member.

Emotional Healing and Self-Care

The journey of single motherhood requires emotional healing and self-care. Sisterhood provides a safe space for single mothers to share their emotions, express vulnerabilities, and seek guidance. The power of listening and validation within this community can be transformative, allowing women to heal and rebuild their lives. Moreover, by promoting self-care practices such as meditation, exercise, and seeking professional help when needed, the community reinforces the importance of taking care of oneself while raising children.

Collaboration and Collaboration

Building a community of single mothers also opens doors for collaboration and collective action. By joining forces, these women can advocate for policies that benefit them and their children, demand equal rights, and challenge social stereotypes. Together, they amplify their voices and create a platform for change. This collective power can inspire policy reform, societal acceptance, and a more inclusive environment for single mothers and their families.

Celebrating Achievements and Milestones

Within a supportive community, single mothers can celebrate their achievements and milestones, no matter how small. Whether it's securing a new job, completing education, or witnessing their children flourish, these victories become shared triumphs. By recognizing and applauding each other's successes, the community reinforces a culture of positivity, resilience, and perseverance, inspiring all members to strive for greatness.

Conclusion

The strength of sisterhood is a transformative force for single mothers. By building a community that nurtures connection, empowers through shared knowledge, breaks the cycle of isolation, promotes emotional healing, encourages self-care, and fosters collaboration, single mothers can embark on their journey of parenthood with renewed vigor and determination. It is through the collective power of sisterhood that these women find the support, understanding, and strength to overcome challenges, celebrate victories, and create a brighter future for themselves and their children. Let us continue to empower single mothers by fostering strong communities that uplift, inspire, and transform lives.

Introduction

Single motherhood is a remarkable journey that involves both triumphs and challenges. It requires resilience, strength, and unwavering dedication. This article celebrates empowered single mothers who defy odds and navigate the complexities of parenting solo. We will explore their triumphs, acknowledge their challenges, and shed light on the remarkable stories that make up the journey of single parenting.

Embracing Independence

Redefining Roles: Single mothers redefine traditional family roles and take on multiple responsibilities. They become the sole providers, nurturers, and decision-makers, defying societal norms and embracing independence.

Building a Support Network: Single mothers often rely on their support networks, including family, friends, and community organizations. The importance of these networks in providing emotional and practical support to help them overcome challenges cannot be overstated.

Financial Stability: Achieving financial stability as a single mother is no small feat. Resourcefulness and determination are demonstrated by single mothers who successfully manage their finances, pursue education, and secure employment opportunities.

Nurturing Resilient Children

Emotional Support: Single mothers become the primary source of emotional support for their children. They face challenges in maintaining a healthy emotional environment while simultaneously dealing with their own emotional needs.

Teaching Life Skills: Single mothers take on the responsibility of teaching essential life skills to their children, from cooking and cleaning to financial literacy and problem-solving. Their dedication in nurturing self-sufficient and resilient individuals is commendable.

Positive Role Models: Single mothers serve as inspiring role models for their children. Through their perseverance and determination, they demonstrate the importance of resilience, hard work, and empathy, shaping the character of their offspring.

Overcoming Challenges

Balancing Work and Parenting: Single mothers often juggle demanding jobs while raising their children. They face challenges in maintaining a work-life balance and employ strategies to ensure their children's well-being.

Battling Stereotypes: Society can sometimes impose unfair stereotypes on single mothers. Prevailing stigmas and biases they encounter are shed light upon, and these strong women challenge and overcome societal expectations.

Self-Care: Self-care is crucial for any parent, particularly for single mothers. They face the challenges of solo parenting and employ various strategies to maintain their well-being.

Celebrating Triumphs

Personal Growth: The journey of single motherhood often fosters personal growth and empowerment. It allows single mothers to discover their strengths, talents, and resilience.

Strong Bonds: Single mothers often develop strong bonds with their children due to the unique circumstances they face. The deep connection that emerges from this shared journey is celebrated, acknowledging the love and support that sustains them.

Success Stories: Highlighting success stories of single mothers who have overcome significant challenges and achieved remarkable accomplishments. These stories inspire and encourage other single mothers to persevere and reach for their dreams.

Conclusion

The journey of single motherhood is a testament to the strength and resilience of empowered women who face the challenges of raising children alone. It encompasses triumphs, growth, and the ability to overcome adversity. Through their unwavering dedication and relentless pursuit of a better future, single mothers empower themselves and their children. As a society, we must celebrate and support these remarkable women, acknowledging their triumphs and recognizing their invaluable contributions.

"Empowering Single Mothers on their Journey" is a poignant and inspiring book that delves into the lives of single mothers, exploring their unique experiences and celebrating their resilience. From unexpected motherhood to embracing independence, this book unravels the challenges faced by unmarried women and widows who navigate the path of single parenthood. It sheds light on the hidden struggles, silent battles, and untold stories of these remarkable women, who break stereotypes and redefine parenthood. With chapters focusing on co-parenting, finances, self-discovery, and community support, this book provides valuable insights, strategies, and encouragement for single mothers, empowering them to embrace their journey with strength and triumph over adversity.

ABOUT THE AUTHOR

Mr. C. P. Kumar is a retired Scientist 'G' from National Institute of Hydrology, Roorkee, Uttarakhand, India. IIc is also a Reiki Healer and Chakra Balancing practitioner (with pendulum dowsing) and offers Emotional Freedom Technique (EFT) to help individuals with emotional issues. Mr. Kumar has authored many books on technical, spiritual, and social topics.

For further details, you may visit his webpage
https://www.angelfire.com/nh/cpkumar/virgo.html

www.ingramcontent.com/pod-product-compliance
Lightning Source LLC
Chambersburg PA
CBHW060952260726
48661CB00005B/1853